THE LEARNING HOUSE

SHEILA E. SAPP

ScarecrowEducation
Lanham, Maryland • Toronto • Oxford
2003

Published in the United States of America
by ScarecrowEducation
An imprint of The Rowman & Littlefield Publishing Group
4501 Forbes Boulevard, Suite 200, Lanham, Maryland 20706
www.scarecroweducation.com

PO Box 317
Oxford
OX2 9RU, UK

British Library Cataloguing in Publication Information Available

Library of Congress Cataloging-in-Publication Data

Sapp, Sheila E.
  The Learning House / Sheila E. Sapp.
      p. cm.
  "A ScarecrowEducation book."
  Includes bibliographical references.
  ISBN 1-57886-022-9 (pbk : alk. paper)
  1. Play. 2. Educational games. 3. Creative activities and seat work.
  4. Early childhood education—Parent participation. 5. Child rearing.
  I. Title.
  HQ782.S333 2003
  649'.51—dc21

                                    2003005523

⊗™ The paper used in this publication meets the minimum requirements of
American National Standard for Information Sciences—Permanence of Paper
for Printed Library Materials, ANSI/NISO Z39.48-1992.
Manufactured in the United States of America

This book is dedicated to my daughter, Nicholyn—"Niki"—who urged me to share my ideas and activities with other parents. I also dedicate this book to my supportive and loving husband, Everette A. Sapp, my encouraging mother, Eva E. Henry, and my maternal grandmother, Ida Victoria Scott Ballance, whom I never knew, who endowed her children with a thirst for knowledge, education, and love for learning.

PURPOSE OF
THE BOOK

The purpose of this resource book is to provide parents with simple activities and strategies to develop, nurture, and enrich readiness skills in reading, mathematics, language, and writing at home. Daycares, home childcare providers, home schoolers, and early childhood educators may also use the book to enhance the offerings and educational experiences provided to children and their families.

CONTENTS

CONTENTS

PREFACE

Thirty years ago, on a warm August morning, I saw my day-old daughter for the first time. She was the most beautiful big-eyed baby and the only girl among the babies born that hot, humid night. The nurse on duty exclaimed as she wheeled my daughter over to me, "Look at her! She's holding her head up and only a day old!" I smiled, proud of my daughter, who already showed an interest in the new and strange world around her.

I felt I already knew this day-old wonder peering curiously at me while sucking hungrily, cradled in my arms. Finally, I actually see the baby I've been reading and reciting nursery rhymes to these past nine months. That August fifth morning marked the beginning of an adventure with learning and discovery for both of us.

During my daughter's early childhood years, we enjoyed many hours of fun-filled learning experiences and activities at home. One evening, years later, after a day at school, I expressed concern about the number of kindergarten and first-grade children who still could not tie their shoes. My daughter replied matter-of-factly, "Make the shoe string tie game you made for me. I still remember that game you made to help me learn how to tie my shoes. Mom, you should put all your ideas together and share your games with other parents."

Nodding my head, I said, "I probably will one day."

ACKNOWLEDGMENTS

I wish to thank Mrs. Betty Fullilove, who reminded me through periodic telephone calls and cards of my task. Her words of support served as a positive impetus and motivator. I wish Betty success with her future endeavors.

I also want to thank the parents I have had the opportunity to work with throughout my thirty-one years as an educator and administrator. The experiences I gained by their participation and cooperation have been invaluable.

1

INTRODUCTION

Parents play an integral role in the early intellectual development and educational growth of their children. Researchers examining the influence of parental involvement on student achievement have found a positive relationship between parental involvement and school success. Families that provide an encouraging learning environment at home and are involved with their children's educational program produce children who succeed academically throughout their schooling years. Many parents are not aware of their powerful influence and the impact they have on the early development of intellectual abilities and learning attitudes of children.

Young children's minds are like sponges, ready to soak up everything in their environment through their senses. They are born with a natural curiosity about the world around them and are anxious to explore, examine, and experience everything within or not within their reach. It is up to us as parents and educators to tap into this reservoir and lead children toward the path of a lifelong love for learning.

By the time children enter preschool or kindergarten, they possess a repertoire of skills, experiences, concepts, and perceptions taught by their parents and/or other significant individuals residing in the home. There is no question that parents are their children's first teachers.

Think back. Who was responsible for teaching your child to talk, to walk, and to perform other simple gross and fine motor activities like hand clapping, holding a cup, or repeating a nursery rhyme? The answer is you! If there is doubt in your mind about your capabilities as a teacher, list everything your child knew or learned prior to going to daycare, preschool, and kindergarten. I guarantee you will run out of time and paper! Children spend more quality learning time with their parents and other significant family members than they do with classroom teachers, daycare, or home care providers.

With a series of simple-to-do activities and the rooms in your house, you are about to embark on a learning adventure that will be both pleasurable and meaningful. This adventure will not require a lot of time or effort, but it will require commitment. All I request of you, or another significant family member in your home, is thirty minutes a day: fifteen minutes in the morning and afternoon or a thirty-minute block of time that fits into your routine and your family's schedule. As your assistant and guide, I will help you convert your home into an active learning laboratory for your child. Are you ready to start our adventure? Good! Let's begin!

2

USING ROOMS AS LEARNING STATIONS

KITCHEN LEARNING STATION

Our first stop during our adventure is the kitchen. Yes, the kitchen. Why? You and your family will spend more time in the kitchen than in any other room of your home. One task required before we begin is to make sure your kitchen is safe and clear of harmful items that might endanger your child's safety. Ensuring the safety and well-being of your child is a matter of making sure the kitchen and other rooms in the house are child-proof. You may accomplish this by moving objects out of the reach of curious little fingers. A simple way to check your kitchen for safety is to get on your knees and slowly scan your kitchen. By doing so, you are at the eye level of three- or four-year-olds. Do you see anything that would attract the attention of your child? Do you have potentially hazardous objects or cleaning supplies in your lower cabinets? Are caps on bottles tight? Once you are satisfied with the results of your safety check, you may open your Kitchen Learning Laboratory.

Reading Readiness Skills

Labeling Objects in the Kitchen (Ages 4–7)

You'll need the following materials to label (name) objects in your kitchen: a black permanent marker, a pack of unlined index cards, a pack of self-applied laminating sheets, and masking or cellophane tape or glue. Note: Laminating the cards will increase their usability and life. Using your best print handwriting, write the names of objects in your kitchen and tape the labeled card on each object chosen. For example, label the stove, refrigerator, sink, table, chair, cabinet, clock, toaster, cupboard, drawer, oven, and other appropriate objects in your kitchen. You can make your labeled word cards even more useful by finding pictures of the objects in your kitchen and pasting them on the word cards. This way, your child will be able to associate the picture of the object with the written word (name) of the object. Adding pictures also makes word cards an excellent activity for children learning to speak English.

Kitchen Tour (Ages 3–4)

Three- and four-year-olds will love this tour of the kitchen! Take your child by the hand and point to each object in the kitchen. Tell him or her the name of the object and briefly explain the purpose of the object or item in the kitchen.

Naming Labeled Objects in the Kitchen (Ages 4–7)

Set aside fifteen minutes each day to say the name of selected objects in the kitchen with your child. Initially, start off with naming and pointing to three to five kitchen objects. Lead your child by the hand and say the name of the object distinctly and clearly. Follow the procedure specified below for every labeled object in your kitchen.

Point to the object and say the name of the object. Repeat the name of the object as you point to the word card. Have your child say the name of the object and point to the word card. If you have pictures on the word card, point to the picture and ask, "Do you know what this is a picture of?" Note: If your child does not respond correctly, simply tell him or her the name of the object. Say the name of the picture. Point to the word that names the picture.

Alternate Activities for the Labeled Word Cards

Picture Word Card Match (Ages 3-5) Materials Needed: scissors, oak tag or cardboard, glue, and pictures.

Directions: Using old magazines, sales advertisements, or catalogs, cut out pictures of objects labeled in your kitchen. Paste the pictures on an 8.5" × 11" oak tag or cardboard. Make as many game boards as you need to accommodate the number of objects in your kitchen. Encourage your child to respond in a complete sentence. You model how you want your child to respond by doing the first two items with him or her. For example, say: "This is a refrigerator. Where is the refrigerator?" Ask your child to find the refrigerator in your kitchen. Follow this procedure until your child has identified all of the pictured objects. Note: Six- and seven-year-olds may point to the word and say the name of each letter in the word "refrigerator." After naming the letters (spelling) in the word, instruct your child to say the word (refrigerator) aloud. The steps are: say the word, spell the word, and say the word.

Language Activities

What Am I Doing? (Ages 3-7)   Talk about what you are doing in the kitchen out loud (washing dishes, baking a cake, setting the table, and so forth). Encourage your child to say what you are doing in his or her own words. Note whether or not your child uses complete sentences. Write down the words that are mispronounced. Help your child learn how to say mispronounced words. As a follow-up activity, have your child draw a picture about something he or she has seen you do in the kitchen. Ask your child to tell you what you are doing in the picture.

Tell Me the Sequence (Ages 3-4)   Directions: Briefly tell your child what you are doing out loud as you perform little tasks in the kitchen. Say: "I am going to sweep the kitchen floor. First, I need to get the broom to sweep the floor. Next, I am going to sweep the floor. Then, I am going to get the dustpan to pick up the trash on the floor. After I pick up the trash with the dustpan, I am going to put the trash in the trash pail/can." This procedure may be used with other activities in the kitchen.

Tell Me the Sequence (Ages 5-7)   Questions you may ask five- to seven-year-olds using the same procedure outlined above are as follows:

1. "What did I do first?"
2. "What happened next?"
3. "What was the last thing I did?"

Or, ask your child to draw a picture showing the sequence of the events or activities taking place in the kitchen.

Sequence Match (Ages 6-7)   Materials Needed: Picture Word Match Game Board, a black crayon, an old magazine, scissors, and glue.

Directions: Using the black crayon, write "First," "Second," and "Third" at the top of each box starting from left to right. Have your child find pictures in a magazine to show what happened first, second, and third. The pictures must be glued in the appropriate box.

CHAPTER 2

PICTURE WORD MATCH GAME BOARD

Letter Recognition and Identification (Ages 4-7) Using the same word cards, name different objects in the kitchen, pointing from left to right. Say the name of the first letter of the object. For example, say "Table—T." Have your child say the name of the letter after you name each letter. To see if your child can identify and recognize the letter "T" in different settings, ask your child to point to, circle, or underline the letter "T" in old magazines, newspapers, books, and advertisements. This same activity may be used with all the objects labeled in your kitchen.

I Spy a Letter (Ages 3-5) Materials Needed: Two empty cereal boxes.

Directions: Put your finger on a letter of your choosing. Say: "I spy a letter. The name of the letter I spied is ____." Have your child say the name of the letter you identified. With your finger still pointing to the letter, ask your child to find the same letter on the other cereal box.

Letter Scrapbook (Ages 5-7) Materials Needed: Sheets of 8.5" × 11" oak tag, construction, or plain white paper, scissors, old newspaper advertisement or magazine, permanent black marker, and glue.

Directions: At the top of each sheet of paper, write one letter (capital and lowercase). Using the newspaper or magazine, have your child find the selected letter in the advertisement or magazine. Cut out the letter and glue it on the paper. Follow this same procedure until you have a page for each letter in the alphabet. Encourage your child to identify and name letters on other appropriate items in your kitchen such as cereal boxes, milk cartons, canned goods, cake mix boxes, and so forth. Note: The letter scrapbook can also be used to glue pictures of objects and words that begin with each selected letter (ages 5-7).

Around and Around I Go (Ages 3-5) You and your child will enjoy this movement activity while learning the names of objects in your kitchen. Stand in the middle of your kitchen with one arm and your pointer finger extended. Slowly turn yourself around while saying, "Around and around I go. Where I stop, does _____ know?" Fill in your child's name in the blank. Each time you turn around point to a different object. Your child must tell you the name of the object specified.

Positional Words (Ages 3-5) Young children love to explore kitchen cabinets. They can spend hours taking pots, pans, and containers out of floor cabinets. Parents can enrich their child's play by teaching "positional" words such as in, out, on, off, up, down, above, and below. Try the activity below with three- to five-year-olds.

Materials Needed: A small pan (optional), rubber ball, or favorite toy (stuffed animal, doll, truck, car).

Directions: Select one of the suggested items from the materials list. Ask your child to put his or her toy *in* the cabinet. Put emphasis on the word "in." If your child does not respond appropriately, take your child's toy and say, "Watch me." Repeat the instruction and show your child how to put the toy in the cabinet. After you have demonstrated (modeled) putting the toy in the cabinet, return the toy to your child and say, "Put the _____ in the cabinet."

Add variety to this learning activity by including movement and naming parts of the body. Direct your child to do the following:

1. "Put your hand on your head."
2. "Take your hand off of your head."
3. "Put your elbow on the table."

4. "Put your hand under your chin."
5. "Put your hand over your head."
6. "Put your finger in your mouth."
7. "Walk out of the kitchen."
8. "Put your foot under the table."
9. "Put your knee on the floor."
10. "Put your arm up."

Positional Words Game Board (On, Off, Above, Below, Top, and Bottom) (Ages 3–6)   Use the Positional Words Game Board to help your child understand the concept of positional words.

Directions: Say: "I am going to tell you to do something with your finger. Listen carefully and do what I say."

1. "Put your finger on the picture of the apple."
2. "Put your finger at the top of the apple."
3. "Put your finger above the apple."
4. "Take your finger off the apple."
5. "Put your finger below the apple."
6. "Put your finger at the bottom of the apple."

POSITIONAL WORDS GAME BOARD

Positional Word Game Variation (Ages 6-7) Materials Needed: A box of crayons and one 8.5" × 11" plain sheet of paper.

Directions: Ask your child to do the following on a plain sheet of paper:

1. "Draw a large circle in the center of the paper."
2. "Draw a hat on top of the circle."
3. "Draw a flower under the circle."
4. "Draw a wagon in the circle."
5. "Draw an 'x' on the wagon."
6. "Draw a flag on the right side of the circle."
7. "Draw a tree on the left side of the circle."
8. "Draw a ball beside the tree."
9. "Draw a triangle above the tree."
10. "Draw a square in the bottom of the circle."

Where is the Pot? (Ages 3-4) Materials Needed: A small or medium-size pot and a small cardboard square or circle.

Directions: Tell your child to do the following with the pot and cardboard square:

1. "Place the pot on the table."
2. "Put the square in the pot."
3. "Hold the pot above your head."
4. "Take the square out of the pot."
5. "Put the pot under the table."
6. "Hold the pot above the sink."
7. "Put the square beside the pot."
8. "Put the pot over the square."
9. "Put the pot on the square."
10. "Hold the square below the pot."

Where Is the Object? (Ages 3–5) You may use the Positional Words Game Board for this activity that is a variation of the previous learning activity.

Materials Needed: A lima bean or any other small object.

Directions: Say: "I have a lima bean in my hand. Watch closely to see where I place the lima bean. I want you to tell me where the lima bean is. Are you ready?"

Put the lima bean on the apple. Say: "Where is the lima bean?" Ask your child to respond by saying, "The lima bean is _____ the apple." Note: Do the first one with your child. Your child must use one of the positional words specified previously.

Positional Words Movement Activity (Open, Close, In, and Out) (Ages 3–6) Materials Needed: An empty cereal box or any other appropriate object.

Directions: Say: "I have an empty cereal box on the kitchen table. Let me see you open the box. Put your hand in the box. Take your hand out of the box. Close the box. Open the kitchen cabinet door. Put the cereal box in the cabinet." This activity also demonstrates whether or not your child can follow one-step directions. You may increase the complexity of this activity by combining the one-step directions. For example, closing the cereal box and putting the box in the cabinet.

Mathematics Readiness Skills

Counting Objects in the Kitchen

All counting activities require parental assistance until your child begins to associate a number with "how many." Start with these simple learning activities in your kitchen.

Count with Me (Ages 3–5) Directions: Holding your child's hand, walk around your kitchen and count objects. Say: "Let's count together to see how many chairs we have in our kitchen." Have your child repeat each number after you as you count. Next, count again together. For example, count the number of windows in your kitchen. "We have one window in our kitchen. Say one after me." Or, "Say one with me. I am holding up one finger. Now, you hold up one finger. You have one nose. Point to your nose. You have one mouth. Point to your mouth. You have one chin. Point to your chin." Then ask, "How many refrigerators do we have? How many stoves do we have? How many tables do we have? How many legs are on our kitchen table? How many handles are on our cabinet doors or drawers? How many pots have handles? How many doors are on our refrigerator? How many slices of bread can we put in our toaster?" Use the same procedure in the example specified above with your child.

Show Me (Ages 4-6) Materials Needed: Five small plastic cups, a paper plate, and five plastic spoons and forks.

Directions: Place the items on your kitchen table. Note: Before you begin the activity, make sure your child recognizes and knows the name of the items for the learning activity. Say: "We are going to play a counting game together using the items on the table. When I tell you to show me an item, I want you to put the item on the paper plate. First, show me . . .

1. two cups
2. one fork
3. two spoons
4. three cups
5. four spoons
6. five cups
7. one spoon
8. five forks."

Alternate Activities (Ages 3–5) Materials Needed: A black permanent marker and a pack of 5" × 7" index cards.

Directions: Using the permanent marker, write the numerals 1–5 (write one numeral on each card) on an index card. Shuffle the cards. Hold up a numeral card. Say: "When I hold up the card with a number, show me how many spoons, cups, or forks to put on the plate." Your child may hold up the appropriate number of fingers to show how many items need to be put on the plate. Note: For ages 6–7, write the numerals 1–20 on index cards. On separate index cards, ask your child to draw triangles or find objects that show "how many" when you hold up a numeral card.

Number Scavenger Hunt (Ages 6–7) Materials Needed: An old magazine, glue, scissors, numeral cards (1–20), and two sheets of 8.5" × 11" white paper.

Directions: Hide the numeral cards around the room. Your child must cut out objects from the magazine that match the numeral card he or she finds.

How Many in the Cup? (Ages 3–5) Materials Needed: A plastic cup, plastic forks and spoons.

Directions: Place a plastic cup on the kitchen table. Using the plastic spoons or forks, place one, two, or three items in the cup. Say: "Tell me how many items are in the cup." Help your child count the selected item in the cup if assistance is needed. Continue this procedure until your child can successfully count the different number of items you place in the plastic cup.

Numeral Card Match (Ages 3–7) Materials Needed: Numeral cards (1–5 or 1–20).

Directions: Say: "I am going to show you a number on a card. I want you to use your fingers to show me how many. Let's do the first one together." Select a numeral card. For example, hold up the number one. Say: "Do you know what number this is? Yes, this is number 'one.' Show me one finger. Good job!"

Remember, when I show you the numeral card, use your fingers to show me how many."

Note: You may vary this activity by asking your child to find items in the kitchen to show you how many. Your child may also clap his or her hands to show how many when the numeral card is presented. As your child progresses, increase the numbers. Five-, six-, and seven-year-olds should be able to count and recognize numbers from one through twenty. Let your child's performance and progress determine pacing and the amount of skills and concepts presented. Remember, you want your child to be successful and develop a love for learning.

Number Book (Ages 4–7)   Materials Needed: Plain white paper (8.5" × 11"), scissors, glue or cellophane tape, an old magazine or advertisement, and a stapler. Optional: Your child may draw pictures to show how many instead of cutting out pictures from a magazine.

Directions: In the center of the top of each page write a number (1–5 or 1–20). In the center of the bottom of the page, write a number word. Have your child find or draw pictures for each number. Add number pages to the number book as your child progresses. See the following sample page.

SAMPLE NUMBER BOOK PAGE

1

(Place picture(s) or drawing(s) in the center.)

One

Straws Egg Carton Counter (Ages 4–7)   Materials Needed: One empty egg carton, a pair of scissors, twenty drinking straws, and a black permanent marker.

Directions: Cut the bottom out of each egg container. Close the egg carton and place the carton on the kitchen table with the holes facing up. Using the black permanent marker, write a number on the front side of each egg section. Point to a number and say: "Tell me how many straws I need to put in this egg section." Direct your child to pick up the number of straws that show how many should be placed in the egg counter. Have your child count the straws out loud before he or she places the straws in the appropriate number egg container.

Lima Beans Egg Carton Counter (Ages 4–7)   Materials Needed: A black permanent marker, an empty egg carton, and a small bag of lima beans.

Directions: Remove the lid from the top of the egg carton. On the inside of the egg section, write the numerals 1–5 (1–10 for ages 5–7) with the black permanent marker. Point to one of the numbers written in the egg carton. Say: "What is this number? Yes this is the number _____." Say: "The number tells us how many lima beans to place in the egg. Let's do the first one together." Count the number of lima beans needed with your child and place the lima beans in the egg. Note: As your child advances, increase the numbers by adding egg cartons.

You may also use the egg carton counter for simple addition and subtraction problems. For example, put five lima beans in number five egg section and put two lima beans in number two egg section. Remove the five lima beans and place them on the table. Next remove the two lima beans and place them on the table. Then, put the two sets of lima beans together. Say: "How many lima beans do we have altogether?" Using the lima beans that are already on the table, take away some lima beans. Say: "I am going to take away three lima beans. How many lima beans are left? Let's count together." Follow this same procedure as you continue to add or subtract. As your child progresses, encourage him or her to make up addition or subtraction problems. Use items already available in your house that are safe for your child to handle.

Egg Carton Addition (Ages 6–7) Materials Needed: An empty egg carton, two lima beans, and a black permanent marker.

Directions: Write the numerals 1–12 on the inside of the egg sections. Do not remove the lid from the egg carton. Place two lima beans in the egg carton. Close the lid. Tell your child to shake the egg carton. Open the egg carton and add the two numbers where the lima beans landed. Your child may write the number combinations on index cards. See if your child can make up simple addition problems using different combinations of the numbers in the egg carton.

How Many Are Left? (Ages 3–5) Materials Needed: Five plastic spoons, forks, or straws and one cup.

Directions: Place five of one of the objects in the cup. Tell your child to count the objects in the cup. Say: "I am going to take two spoons out of the cup. Let's count to see how many are left. Yes, there are three spoons left." Put the two spoons removed back in the cup. Say: "I am going to take four spoons from the cup. How spoons are left?" Say: "Yes, there is one spoon left." Optional: You may use kitchen items such as pots, pans, silverware, or lids for counting objects.

Numeral Cards (Ages 3–7) Materials Needed: A pack of 5" × 7" index cards, macaroni or lima beans, a black permanent marker, and glue.

Directions: Write the numerals 1–5 or 1–10 (ages 5–7) at the top of each card. Say: "We are going to make some number cards together. Look at the number on the card. How many macaroni/ lima beans do we need to put on this card?" Count with your child if assistance is needed. Guide your child with this activity by having him or her say the number and count the number of items to glue on the card.

There are many variations of the previous activities. Do not be afraid to use your own creative ideas to plan learning experiences for your child. As you try several of the activities presented in this chapter, you'll think of other ways to use the game boards and cards with your child. Be willing to experiment! Listed in the back of this book are other resources for developing math and reading skills.

BEDROOM LEARNING STATION

Next to the kitchen, your child will spend as many or maybe even more hours (awake or sleep) in his or her bedroom. Why not add zest to your child's bedtime routine by doing fifteen-minute learning experiences before the lights go out? We will begin with an all-time favorite.

Reading Readiness Skills

Reading a Book (Ages 3–7)

Materials Needed: An age-appropriate picture book or story-book.

Directions: Select a picture book or storybook to read aloud to your child. Make sure you use expression while reading the story aloud. Changing your voice to represent different characters in the story will add excitement to the story. The best position to place your child while reading is in your lap. Depending on the size of your child, decide whether or not you want your child in your lap or in his or her bed. Do the following while reading to your child:

1. Read the title of the picture book or storybook.
2. State the name of the author and illustrator of the story. Briefly explain who the *author* (writes the story) and *illustrator* (draws the pictures) are.
3. Ask your child to look at the book's cover. Say: "What do you see?" Have your child point to the objects he or she sees. Say: "What do you think this story is about?"
4. Point out pictures to your child. See if he or she can name the pictures.
5. Stop periodically throughout the story and ask your child questions. For example, "What do you think will happen next? What is your part of the story? Why?"
6. Move your finger from left to right under the written text.
7. Let your child turn the pages as you read aloud.
8. When reading stories with passages or lines that are repeated, encourage your child to read along with you.
9. Switch roles and let your child "read" to you.
10. Become familiar enough with a story to "tell" it to your child. Use expressive language and appropriate body movements, facial expressions, and gestures during storytelling.

Auditory Discrimination (Sounds) (Ages 4–7)

Directions: Say: "I am going to say two words. Tell me if the words are the same or different. If they are the same, say 'yes.' If they are not the same (different), say 'no.' Are you ready? Let's begin."

1. "bat . . . bat
2. cup . . . cat
3. four . . . feet
4. tip . . . tip
5. tub . . . top
6. sew . . . sew
7. far . . . far
8. hear . . . herd."

Auditory Discrimination (Sounds in the Beginning) (Ages 4–7)

Directions: Read the pairs of words listed below to your child. Tell him or her to listen to the sound in the beginning of each of the words you say. Say, "If the words begin the same, say 'yes.' If the words do not sound the same in the beginning, say 'no.'" Note: You may increase the difficulty level by asking your child to give *you* two words that sound the same in the beginning.

1. "car . . . cat
2. rain . . . wet
3. boat . . . box
4. top . . . toy
5. man . . . nest."

Rhyme Time (Ages 4–7)

Directions: Say: "Some words sound the same at the end. We say they rhyme when they sound alike at the end. For example, listen to these two words: cat . . . hat. Say them with me: cat . . . hat. Cat and hat sound alike at the end. I am going to say some more words. I want you to listen to the sounds at the end. Hold up one finger if you hear the same sounds at the end of the words I say:

1. book . . . look
2. well . . . let
3. mop . . . top
4. fan . . . can
5. sun . . . run
6. cake . . . lake
7. toe . . . goat
8. see . . . bee
9. tie . . . pie
10. wall . . . ball."

Rhyming Riddles Time or "I Am Thinking Of . . ." (Ages 5–7)

Directions: Say: "I am going to play a rhyming riddle game with you. I will give you a clue. The answer will rhyme with the clue I give you. Listen to this riddle. I am thinking of a word that rhymes with nap and it's something you wear on your head. What word am I thinking of? The word is cap. Cap rhymes with nap. A cap is worn on the head. Let's try some other rhyming riddles."

1. "I am thinking of a word that rhymes or sounds like door at the end and your bed is on it. What word am I thinking of?" (Answer: floor.)
2. "I am thinking of a word that rhymes with red and it's what you sleep on. What word am I thinking of?" (Answer: bed.)
3. "I am thinking of something you put on your foot before your shoe that rhymes with clock. What word am I thinking of?" (Answer: sock.)

4. "I am thinking of a word that rhymes with willow and it's something you put your head on. What word am I thinking of?" (Answer: pillow.)
5. "I am thinking of a word that rhymes with sight. You turn it on in your bedroom when it's dark. What word am I thinking of?" (Answer: light.)

Rhyming Picture Cards Matching (Ages 5–7)

Materials Needed: A pack of 5" × 7" index cards, an old magazine or advertisement page, scissors, and glue.

Directions: Find pictures of items that rhyme. Glue each selected object on each index card. Shuffle the cards and place them face down on your child's bed. Say: "Turn the cards over one at a time. See if you can find pictures of objects that rhyme."

Nursery Rhyme Time (Ages 4–7)

Directions: Recite a familiar nursery rhyme (such as "Jack and Jill") to your child. Have your child tell you the words that rhyme as you say or read a nursery rhyme. Note: Dr. Seuss books are excellent for teaching the concept of rhyming or hearing rhyming words.

Tell Me a Rhyming Word (Ages 5–7)

Materials Needed: Rhyming picture cards.

Directions: Say: "I am going to hold up one of the rhyming picture cards. I want you to tell me a word that rhymes with the picture I have in my hand." Encourage your child to think of as many words as possible that rhyme with each selected picture.

Naming Objects I Sound or Spell (Auditory Blending) (Ages 4–5)

Directions: Select items in the bedroom. Divide the names of the objects into sounding parts. For example, book. Pronounce "b" (sound of the letter b) and "ook." Repeat the sounds twice. Then ask your child to tell you the word you said. Note: If your child experiences difficulty with this activity, select three items in the bedroom and place them on the bed. Sound out the name of an item. See if your child can point to the item he or she heard you say. Say: "Listen to what I say carefully. I am going to name some objects in the room by saying the sounds. I want you to tell me the object I am saying. Are you ready to begin?"

1. door—"d" "oor"
2. lamp—"l" "amp"
3. bed—"b" "ed"
4. blanket—"blan" "ket"

Bedtime Positional Words Activity (Ages 3–7)

Directions: Say: "I am going to tell you some things to do. Let's see how well you listen."

1. "Sit on the bed."
2. "Put your head under the pillow."
3. "Pull the covers over your head."
4. "Close your eyes."
5. "Put your slippers under the bed."
6. "Hang your bathrobe in your closet."
7. "Hold your pillow above your head."

8. "Turn the light off."
9. "Put your hand on top of the covers."
10. "Open your closet door."

Color Word Cards (Ages 5–7)

Materials Needed: A pack of 5" × 7" index cards, crayons or colored pencils, and a black permanent marker.

Directions: Write each of the following color words on an index card with the black permanent marker: red, blue, black, green, yellow, orange, brown, and purple. Using crayons or colored pencils, draw a circle and fill in the center with the color that matches the color word. You may add additional color words after your child has learned to recognize and identify the eight basic colors.

Say: "I am going to hold up a color word card. Say the name of the color. Find two things in your bedroom that are the same color." Increase the number of items to find and colors as your child progresses.

LIVING AND FAMILY ROOMS AS LEARNING STATIONS

The living and family rooms are very popular gathering places for family members as well as friends. Parents and children gather to relax, watch television, and play board games. Take advantage of your family gatherings and the activities taking place while you enjoy each other. Everyone has a stake in broadening and developing your child's skills. Below are some activities to try that require no materials and very little time.

Reading and Mathematics Readiness Skills (Ages 5–7)

1. See how many items your child can name in five minutes in your living or family room. Make picture word cards for the items your child was unable to name correctly.
2. Have your child point to the furniture in the room.
3. Have your child count and show with his or her fingers the number of chairs and tables in the room. Also, ask your child to count the number of legs on the tables and chairs.
4. Have your child count the number of buttons or knobs on the television (if applicable). Ask your child to turn the television or radio on and off.
5. Let your child count and add the dots on both dice while playing a board game. Note: Games that require children to count spaces for moves provide excellent practice for counting.
6. Choose a color. Ask your child to find items that match the color you selected.
7. Name two items in the room that begin with the same sound as the restaurant "McDonald's."
8. Ask your child to tell you how many adults (big people) and children (little people) are in the room.
9. Write the names of items in the room. Ask your child to say the name of the letters in the words.
10. After your child has finished watching his or her television show, ask the child to draw a picture of his or her favorite part of the story.
11. Draw a shape such as a circle, square, or triangle on a sheet of plain white paper. Point to the shape you selected and tell your child to find items in the room that have the same shape.

12. Make up riddles for your child to solve that involve objects, items, and activities in the room. For example, "I am thinking of something in the room that tells us the time. What am I thinking of?"

13. Use card games to help your child identify and match, colors, numbers, shapes, and letters.

14. An old deck of playing cards may be used for sorting (hearts, diamonds, clubs, spades) and making simple addition and subtraction (take away) problems to solve.

15. Have your child talk about or tell you what he or she sees when looking at pictures in magazines or catalogs. Pictures are worth a thousand words!

16. Pantomime (act out) actions such as combing or brushing your hair, eating, washing dishes, reading a book, and so forth. Ask your child to guess what you are doing. Encourage your child to respond in complete sentences. The whole family can take part in this activity.

17. Describe an object or piece of furniture in your living or family room. Ask your child to tell you the name of the object you are describing.

18. Ask your child to pretend that he or she is one of the objects in the room. For example, a television. "What do you think a television would say to a radio? To another television?"

19. "Who is the tallest person in the room? Who is the smallest person in the room? Are you taller than the table, lamp, or coffee table?"

20. "How many windows are in the room?"

21. "How many people can sit on the sofa?"

22. "Who arrived first? Who arrived last?"

23. Have your child count the number of steps it takes to walk across the room.

24. Have your child count how many times the telephone rings.
25. Have your child count the number of pillows in the room.

You may modify many of these activities to use with three- and four-year-olds too. Remember, the key to what you do is your child. Additionally, these activities are meaningful as well as fun for the entire family.

3

EXTRAORDINARY HOUSEHOLD CHORES AND FAMILY ACTIVITIES

Add pizzazz to everyday household tasks! How? It's as easy as one, two, three! Turn ordinary chores into extraordinary learning experiences and opportunities for your child. We'll brighten the prospect of performing household chores by changing your perspective and purpose. You'll not only complete little jobs around your house, but you'll also help develop skills and build concepts, too.

Washing and Drying Dishes (Ages 4–7)   Your child can:

- Sort and match plates, pans, pots, silverware, cups, glasses, and bowls.
- Count plates, cups, silverware, pans, pots, and bowls washed or dried.
- Compare the sizes of plates and saucers.
- Compare the lengths of spoons, forks, and knives.
- Compare the amount of water a cup and glass hold.
- Name items that are used for drinking liquids.
- Name items that are used to assist with eating.
- Name foods we use a fork to eat.

○ Name foods we use a spoon to eat.

○ Name dishes that are shaped like a circle.

○ Count the number of prongs on a fork.

○ Tell you why a cup has a handle.

○ Match cups with saucers.

○ Tell you where to place the dried dishes.

○ Fold a dishtowel in half.

○ Tell you what was washed first and last.

○ Name something that rhymes with spoon.

○ Stack assorted sizes of pans, pots, and bowls.

○ Place the assorted sizes of bowls, pots, and pans in order from the largest to the smallest or the smallest to the largest.

○ Point to the pots and pans used for cooking foods on the stove.

○ Point to the pots and pans used for baking food in the oven.

○ Guess the number of spoons and forks that will fit in a glass.

Setting the Table (Ages 3-7)   Your child can:

Tell you how many dishes to put on the table.

Count the number of napkins, knives, spoons, forks, and glasses needed.

Place silverware on the right (knife and spoon) and left (fork) of the plate.

Place napkins *under* forks on the table.

Trace the outside of the dishes and silverware.

Stand on the right and left side of the plate.

Tell how many dishes and how much silverware are needed based on the number of people eating.

Count the number of sides on the table.

Describe the shape of the table.

Fold the napkins into halves, thirds, and triangles.

Stand at the "head" of the table.

Laundry (Ages 3-4) Directions: Hold up a sock. Say: "Look at this sock. Find the other sock that looks like this one." You may increase the difficulty level by including colors.

Laundry (Ages 5-7) Your child can:

Sort clothes by colors (white clothes, dark clothes).

Sort clothes by functions (play clothes, bedclothes, underwear, and so on).

Sort clothes by classification (towels, shirts, socks, sheets, washcloths, and pants).

Classify clothes by patterns (dots, stripes, checkered, diamonds, squares, and circles).

Match clothes by sets (pants and shirts, towels, washcloths, dishtowels, sheets, socks, and pillowcases).

Sort shirts by short and long sleeves.

Separate shirts with buttons from shirts without buttons.

Count the number of buttons on a parent's dress shirts.

Count the number of belt loops on a pair of pants.

Folding and Putting Clothes Away (Ages 4-7) Your child can:

Match socks and put them together.

Find clothing shaped like squares or rectangles.

Count the number of pairs of socks each person in the family has.

- Place the folded items in the correct person's room or dresser.
- Classify the clothes by function and activity.
- Point to the top, middle, and bottom drawer on a dresser.
- Draw a picture of clothes he or she wears to church, to school, outside, and to bed.
- Make stacks of two shirts and three shirts.
- Match a pair of socks to a pair of shoes.
- Separate clothes that have pockets and zippers.
- Sort clothes by their texture (rough or soft, smooth or bumpy).

Dusting Furniture (Ages 5-7)   Your child can:

- Count the objects removed from the furniture before dusting.
- Tell you where to put the objects removed.
- Tell you in what order the objects were removed.
- Draw a picture showing the order of steps used to dust.
- Name the objects moved for dusting.
- Practice writing the numerals 1–5 in the dust.

Buying Groceries (Ages 4-7)   Trips to the grocery store can be fun as well as educational for your child! Your child can:

- Tell you the aisle numbers.
- Tell you why some items are in refrigerated containers.
- Name the items in the grocery store (apples, oranges, and so on).

- Tell you the color of items you specify.
- Select the number of canned goods you request.
- Compare the different sized cans, jars, boxes, and bottles in the store.
- Count the number of people you pass in the aisles while shopping.
- Point to items located on the top, middle, and bottom of a shelf.
- Name items and objects that start with specified letters or sounds.
- Name foods that rhyme (potato/tomato).
- Classify foods by naming and pointing to vegetables, fruits, meats, breads, juices, and so on.
- Point to items that are cooked on the stove or in the oven.
- Name grocery items that are eaten cold.
- Name grocery items that must be cooked or baked before eaten.
- Count the number of cookies, cakes, and vegetables contained in clear packages.
- Count the number of apples, potatoes, oranges, and grapefruits in a bag.
- Count the number of purchases placed on the counter from your shopping cart.
- Match pictures of foods on advertisement bulletins with the actual items in the store.
- Find and read the words "enter," "exit," "women," and "men" on doors.
- Show you where you would find butter, milk, or eggs.
- Tell you which item has more or less than another item (one dozen of eggs or a package with six muffins).

Putting Groceries Away (Ages 3-7)   The entire family can pitch in and help with this household chore! While helping you put away groceries, your child can:

- Show or tell you where to put the items purchased from the grocery store.
- Sort the items (canned goods, boxes, bags, and packages).
- Separate canned fruits from canned vegetables.
- Tell you which items should be placed in the refrigerator or cabinet.
- Count the number of canned goods.
- Tell you the names of the items purchased.
- Count the total number of purchases.
- Tell you the order in which the groceries were put away.
- Place canned goods and boxes in order according to their size.
- Count the number of peaches in a can.
- Count the number of pickles in a jar.
- Count the number of bags (paper or plastic) needed to carry your groceries.
- Count the number of times you put items in the refrigerator and cabinet.
- Fold paper bags and tell you the sequence (order) used to fold the bags.
- Name letters and numbers printed on grocery bags (if applicable).
- Point to numbers specified on your grocery receipt(s).
- Name the grocery items as you put them away.
- Open and close the refrigerator and cabinet doors or drawers as grocery items are put away.

Washing Windows (Ages 4–7) While brightening the view of the world outside, your child can:

- Count the number of windowpanes in your windows (if applicable).
- Point to the windowpane in the middle, on the right side, and on the left side of the window.
- Point to the top and bottom of the window.
- Name the objects and items seen while looking out the window.
- Clean an imaginary windowpane by making small circles with his or her hand toward the right (clockwise).
- Clean an imaginary windowpane by making small circles with his or her hand toward the left (counterclockwise).
- Push the window up and pull the window down.
- Count the number of windows in the house and tell you which room has the most windows.
- Draw a picture showing the sequence (steps) for washing the windows.
- Name the parts of the window (windowpane, windowsill, window shade, and curtains/blinds).

Making Sandwiches (Ages 4–7) Your child can:

- Tell you how many slices of bread are needed to make a sandwich.
- Count how many sandwiches are needed, depending on the number of family members.
- Count how many pieces you have if a sandwich is cut in halves, thirds, or fourths.

🍞 Count the number of slices of bread in the loaf of bread before the sandwiches are made.

🍞 Tell you how many slices of bread are left in the loaf of bread after the sandwiches are made.

Baking Cookies (Ages 3–7) For a simple, middle-of-the-day activity or late evening treat, bake chocolate chip cookies using your favorite slice-and-bake cookie brand. Your child can:

🧁 Count the cookies as they're placed on the cookie sheet.

🧁 Count the number of chocolate chips in each cookie.

🧁 Estimate (guess) how many cookies will fill a cookie jar (ages 5–7).

🧁 Cut the cookie dough in halves, thirds, or fourths using a butter knife.

🧁 Solve simple cookie mathematics problems. For example, if you have five cookies and eat three cookies, how many cookies are left?

🧁 Name the objects used to make the cookies.

Making Bread, Dinner Rolls, or Biscuits (Ages 3–7) While you are busy preparing for dinner, set aside extra dough so your child can learn while you work. Your child can:

🍞 Knead and roll the dough with his or her hands.

🍞 Make letters, shapes, and numbers with the dough.

🍞 Divide the dough into parts (halves, thirds, and fourths).

🍞 Make simple objects out of the dough (hat, kite, and ball).

Mopping, Waxing, Vacuuming, and Dusting Floors (Ages 4-7) Add a little zest to these mundane chores by giving them another purpose. While watching you mop, vacuum, wax, or dust your floors, your child can:

- Count the number of times you go across the floor with your mop, dust broom, vacuum cleaner, or waxer.
- Count the number of times you rinse or wring your mop.
- Tell you the sequence (order) of the steps needed to complete the task.
- Tell you or draw a picture describing what you were doing.
- Tell you why you need to wash, wax, vacuum, or dust floors.
- Name the items needed to mop, vacuum, wax, and dust floors.
- Name rooms in your house that are only vacuumed or mopped.
- Count the number of steps you take while vacuuming or mopping the floor.

Three-year-olds will gain meaningful experiences from these activities by talking about what is taking place while performing the tasks. As your three-year-old matures intellectually, try several of the activities specified in this chapter. Do, however, modify and adjust the activities to meet the performance of your child. Younger children need to be continuously immersed in language. Always talk about what you're doing and tell why you're performing different tasks around your house. Watch the vocabulary of your three-year-old grow! Chapter 4 will provide you with ideas for developing instructional games made of household items to use with your child at home.

4

HOMEMADE
INSTRUCTIONAL GAMES

Malls and stores are bursting at the seams with instructional games, toys, books, workbooks, and other items to improve or develop reading and mathematics readiness at home. Despite all the commercial products on the market, nothing takes the place of games parents can make out of items in the home. Children feel very special using toys, games, and other items made especially for them by their parents or other significant relatives in the family. The following instructional games are not all definitive. As you try several of the game activities, you may see other uses for the game. Feel free to experiment with and expand or extend the activities presented. I expect you, as well as your child(ren), to grow and develop during this exciting educational journey.

"I Can" Can (Ages 3-7)   Empty soup and vegetable cans are handy items to save for use around the house. There are a variety of learning activities for which they can be used. All children love to receive positive strokes or pats on the back for their accomplishments or successes. You can provide a visual reminder of your child's success by making an "I Can" can for your child. Follow the simple steps outlined.

Materials Needed: An empty can, construction paper or adhesive paper, a pack of 5" × 7" unlined or lined index cards, and a black permanent marker.

Directions: Clean and dry the can thoroughly. Cover the outside of the can with construction or adhesive paper. Note: Adhesive paper is easier to use and more durable than construction paper. With a black permanent marker, write "I Can" on the outside of the can. Cut the index cards into small sentence strips. On each strip write: I can _____. Each time your child successfully completes a task or learns a skill, complete the "I can" sentence strip by adding the task or skill learned. For example, "I can *count to ten*" or "I can *tie my shoelaces.*" Tell your child that the "I Can" can is a very special can. Say: "Together, we are going to keep up with all the things you can do. Every time you learn something, I am going to write what you learned on the 'I can' sentence strip and place it in our special 'I Can' can. Let's see if we can fill your 'I Can' can!"

Note: Uses for the "I Can" can are almost unlimited. You and your child will enjoy filling the can with accomplishments. This visual representation of acquired skills serves as a motivator and positive reinforcement of learning. Encourage your child to share his or her "I Can" accomplishments with relatives and friends. Watch your child's confidence and self-esteem blossom!

Homemade Puzzles (Ages 3–7) Instead of purchasing costly puzzles, you can make your own. If there are older siblings in your family, enlist their help. Learning is a family affair!

Materials Needed: One empty cereal box (medium size), scissors, glue, an old magazine, storybook, or coloring book, and one 10" × 13" brown clasp envelope. Optional: Two sheets of 8.5" × 11" laminating sheets.

Directions: Remove the waxed paper from inside the empty cereal box. Cut out the front and back of the cereal box. Discard the remaining cereal box sections. Select a picture for your puzzle from the magazine, storybook, or coloring book. Note: Select a simple picture (few details and action) for younger children (ages 3–5). Older children (ages 5–7) may color the picture selected from the coloring book before gluing the picture. Glue the picture on the inside of one cereal box side (the side with the print and picture should be facing away from you). Optional: After gluing the picture, cover the front and back of the puzzle with the laminating sheets to increase the durability and life of the puzzle. Cut the puzzle into *large* sections. Instruct your child to put the puzzle together on top of the remaining cereal box side (work area). After the puzzle is put together, ask your child to tell you what he or she sees or what is happening in the puzzle. Place the completed puzzle in the clasp envelope. Your child may take the homemade puzzles to the doctor's office or on short family trips.

Shoebox Sorter (Ages 5–7) Materials Needed: A shoebox and assorted size buttons.

Directions: Save buttons from old clothes and place them in a shoebox. Your child may sort the buttons by size, color, and description (buttons with or without holes, flat buttons, and so on). Buttons also make excellent counting tools. Encourage your child to count the number of buttons in each sorting category (size, color, description).

Numeral Card Rings (Ages 3–7) Materials Needed: A pack of 3" × 5" unlined index cards, a one-hole punch, yarn or ribbon, a black permanent marker, a box of crayons, and lima beans (optional).

Directions: Write a numeral near the top of each numeral card. Below the numeral draw dots to show how many. Instead of drawing dots, you may glue lima beans to show how many. Punch a hole in the top of the card. String the numeral cards together with yarn or ribbon. You can make numeral card rings for the numerals 1–5, 1–10, and 1–20. For children ages 5–7, write the numeral word on the back of each number card as an added feature. Older children enjoy making their own numeral rings.

Shoebox Counters (Ages 3-7)   Materials Needed: An empty shoebox, yarn, macaroni, and a one-hole punch.

Directions: Punch a hole on each side of the shoebox. Note: You need to extend a strip of yarn the length of the shoebox. String ten pieces of macaroni on the yarn. Attach the string on each side of the shoebox. Knot the ends of the yarn to keep the yarn from slipping through the punched holes. (See Appendix 1.) Your child may use the counter to perform simple addition and subtraction problems (ages 5–7) or practice counting (ages 3–4).

For example, ask your child to slide two macaroni pieces to the left side of the shoebox. Then ask your child to slide three more pieces of macaroni to the left side of the shoebox. Say: "Count and tell me how many pieces of macaroni you have altogether." As your child progresses, add additional macaroni and strings. Encourage six- and seven-year-old children to make up their own addition and subtraction problems. They may write the problems on index cards to make flash cards. They'll have fun learning basic addition and subtraction facts with flash cards.

Tactile Number and Letter Paper Plates (Ages 3-7)   Materials Needed: Paper plates, a pencil, glue, and one two-pound bag of uncooked rice.

Directions: In the center of each paper plate, write the numerals 1–5 or 1–10 or the letters of the alphabet in pencil. Using the white glue, trace the numerals or letters. Sprinkle rice on each numeral or letter and let the glue dry. Blow or brush away any excess rice. When using the tactile numeral or letter plates with your child, use the procedure specified below:

1. Say the name of the numeral or letter.
2. Ask your child to say the name of the numeral or letter after you.
3. Trace the numeral or letter with your finger. Demonstrate for your child.
4. Tell your child to trace the numeral or letter with his or her finger.
5. Say the name of the numeral or letter.

Six- and seven-year-old children may help you make their numeral or letter plates as a craft project. This same activity may be used to help children learn number words, color words, assigned spelling words, and sight words. Regardless of the age group, children should follow three basic steps—Say, Touch, and Say.

Tying (Making a Bow) and Lacing Shoes (Ages 4–7) Materials Needed: An old tennis shoe (with laces), one 8.5" × 11" piece of cardboard, scissors, and a stapler.

Directions: Cut out the lacing section of the tennis shoe. Allow enough area around the lacing section to provide enough room for stapling. Staple the lacing section to the cardboard. Your child may spend time practicing lacing, unlacing, tying (making a bow), and untying his or her shoes. This tying board is the perfect companion for traveling and other little trips. Watch your child develop fine and gross motor skills! (See Appendix 2.)

Buttoning, Ripping, Snapping, Looping, and Hooking (Ages 3–7) Save old or outgrown shirts, skirts, pants, blouses, and tops to provide practice for the fine and gross motor skills.

Materials Needed: Scissors, a pack of 8.5" × 11" cardstock or cardboard paper, and a stapler.

Directions: Cut out the section around buttons, a zipper, a snap, a button with a loop, and an eyehook. Staple each item on one sheet of cardboard or cardstock paper. To keep the items together, place them in a file folder or large envelope. Note: Baby clothes purchased from yard sales or secondhand stores may be used to provide practice on your child's favorite doll or stuffed toy.

Sound Blending Paper Plates (Ages 3-7) Materials Needed: One 9" paper plate, six brass paper fasteners, two sheets of 8.5" × 11" yellow construction paper, chick heads (three for each paper plate half), scissors, and a black permanent marker.

Directions: Cut the paper plate in half. On the outside of one half of the paper plate, write the word ending "at." Write the word ending "all" on the remaining paper plate half. Using the chick head pattern provided in Appendix 3, trace and cut out six chick heads (three for each paper plate half). For the "at" paper plate half, write the consonant letters "m," "b," and "c" in the center of each chick head. For the "all" paper plate half, write the consonant letters "t," "h," and "w" in the center of the remaining chick heads. Using the brass fasteners, attach the chick heads to the appropriate paper plate. (See Appendix 3.)

Pull up one chick head and say the sound of the consonant letter for your child. Next, say the word ending "at." Say the consonant letter sound and word ending again. Ask your child to say the word you sounded. Repeat as many times as needed. Optional: You may find pictures and glue them on index cards. Tell your child to point to the picture of the word he or she heard. This alternate activity is recommended for children ages 3–5.

You might also tell your child to use the word in a sentence to check their understanding of the word and its use.

Milk Carton Numeral, Word, or Letter Sounds Bank (Ages 3–7) Materials Needed: An empty milk carton (any size), a pack of unlined 5" × 7" index cards, and a black (fine tip) permanent maker.

Directions: Clean the empty milk carton and let it stand overnight to dry. Cut a slot on the side of the milk carton. On index cards, use the permanent marker to write letters of the alphabet, sight words (for six- and seven-years-olds), numerals words, color words, and numerals (1–10, 1–20, 1–50). Each time your child learns one of the above items, place the index card in the bank. Make a milk carton bank for each area listed and watch the bank grow! Children ages six and seven may make sentences and stories using the words in their word banks. Three- to five-year-olds may practice letter sounds by naming objects in the house beginning with the sound represented by the letter on the index card. The letter card may be placed in the bank after your child has demonstrated an understanding of the concept.

Paper Plate Clock (Ages 5–7) Materials Needed: A 9" paper plate, one sheet of black construction paper, one brass paper fastener, and a black crayon or permanent marker.

Directions: Write the numerals 1–12 on the paper plate like the face of a clock. Cut out two arrows resembling the "hands" of the clock. Use the clock to show your child the times his or her favorite cartoon or program comes on television. Tell and show your child the position of the clock's "hands" for the hour. Say: "We eat dinner at six o'clock. This is how the clock looks at six o'clock. The long hand is on the twelve and the short hand is on the six." Point out the time for different activities throughout the day (bedtime, lunchtime, birthday parties, and the like).

Playing Cards (Ages 3-7)   Materials Needed: One deck of playing cards.

Directions: Use an old deck of cards for your child to count, match and name colors, numbers, and shapes. The cards may also be used to help your child perform simple addition and subtraction problems. For example, give your child five cards and ask him or her to place two cards on the table. Then ask him or her to tell you how many cards are left in his or her hand. Or, give your child four cards and ask how many more cards he or she needs to have six cards.

Calendars (Ages 3-7)   Materials Needed: One calendar and lima beans for counters.

Directions: You can use a calendar to teach the days of the week, the months of the year, and number recognition. Using the lima beans, instruct your child (ages 5-7) to put his or her lima bean on the number that comes after seven or move the lima bean three spaces after the seven and say the name of the number that is three spaces after the seven. Also circle holidays and birthdays of family members.

Clothes Hanger Counters (Ages 3-7)   Materials Needed: Clothes hangers, a pack of unlined 5" × 7" index cards, one bag of clip clothespins, a black permanent marker, and a stapler.

Directions: Fold an index card and staple it to the top portion of the hanger. Using the black permanent marker, write a numeral on the front of the card. For example, write the numeral "six." Tell your child to clip six clothespins on the bottom of the hanger. Note: Children can do simple addition and subtraction problems (ages 4-7) by putting hangers together and adding or subtracting (taking away) clothespins. (See Appendix 4.)

Story Books (Ages 3-7)   Materials Needed: Old magazines, books, calendars, and postcards, a pack of 8.5" × 11" assorted colored construction paper, scissors, a stapler or brass paper fasteners, glue, and a black permanent marker.

Directions: Select pictures from a magazine to tell a short story. Glue a picture on each sheet of construction paper. Use a stapler or brass paper fasteners to put the "storybook" together. Tell your child to look at the picture and tell you what he or she sees. Below each picture, use the permanent marker to write (print) what your child says in a complete sentence. Read what your child dictated aloud while pointing to each word read. Note: Point to the words from left to right. Demonstrate how pages are turned with your storybook. Children ages six and seven may write their own stories and draw pictures.

5

SEASONAL AND
HOLIDAY FUN

Seasonal activities and holiday celebrations are perfect opportunities to develop reading and mathematics skills as well as to promote family togetherness. Children love the laughter and gaiety that fill the house as family members prepare for seasonal changes and holiday gatherings. Try the activities outlined in this chapter to add wonder to those special times of the year.

August and September Follies (Ages 3-7) While braving cool weather and crisp air, your child can:

- Collect fallen leaves and compare sizes, shapes, and colors with your assistance.
- Match the leaves that are the same size and color.
- Arrange the leaves according to their sizes (largest to the smallest or smallest to the largest).
- Name the colors of the leaves.
- Name items of clothing worn to play outside when it is cold (winter), hot (summer), and rainy.
- Describe the sound of leaves crushed in his or her hands.

October Fantasies (Ages 3-7)   Your little Halloween goblin can:

🎃 Name the shapes in a carved pumpkin.

🎃 Name the parts of the jack-o-lantern's face (eyes, nose, mouth, eyebrows, and teeth).

🎃 Carve a pumpkin (with assistance) and cut out the parts for the face.

🎃 Count the seeds in the pumpkin.

🎃 Use pumpkin seeds for counters.

🎃 Describe a pumpkin using complete sentences.

🎃 Draw a picture of a pumpkin and name the shapes used to make the pumpkin's face.

🎃 Sort the candy received in his or her treat bag by color, size, and shape.

🎃 Guess the number of candy corns in a bag of candy.

🎃 Count the number of days until Halloween.

🎃 Name the day of the week and the month in which Halloween is celebrated.

🎃 Tell the name of the month that comes before Halloween.

🎃 Say the name of the letter sound heard at the beginning of the word Halloween.

🎃 Find pictures of five objects in a magazine that begin with the same letter sound as Halloween.

🎃 Make a jack-o-lantern. (See Appendix 5.)

Winter Wonderland Fun (Ages 4-7)   Your child can:

 Compare the size of footprints in the snow.

 Build a snowman and name the parts (head, arms, eyes, nose, and mouth).

Describe the feeling of snow.

Place a cup outside and see how long it takes to fill up with snow or rain.

Name items covered with snow in the backyard or in the front lawn/yard.

Draw a picture showing the weather outside and tell what he or she sees.

Find pictures in magazine showing winter, spring, fall, and summer scenes. Compare the pictures.

Name his or her favorite time of the year and tell why (ages 6–7).

November and December Frolics (Ages 4–7) As you welcome the holiday season, your child can:

Determine the number of place settings needed for Thanksgiving dinner.

Count the number of plates, knives, forks, spoons, napkins, and glasses needed to set the table.

Draw a Turkey Hand. (See Appendix 6.)

Name five things he or she is thankful for.

Arrange dinner guests according to height.

Draw a picture showing what he or she wants to have for Thanksgiving dinner.

Count the number of houses on your street with holiday lights.

Sort holiday ornaments by color and shape.

Separate gift packages by names.

Count the number of holiday lights or ornaments on the decorations in your house.

Make holiday cards for family members and relatives (adult assistance is needed).

♥ Create custom gift wrapping paper by decorating brown paper bags with crayons or assorted magic markers or colored pencils.

♥ Count the number of days before the family's winter holiday.

♥ Decorate cookies and count how many cookies are in a dozen.

♥ Estimate the number of cookies made from frozen cookie mix.

♥ Describe a Christmas tree or a Menorah using complete sentences.

♥ Find and name five objects in the house that begin like the words Christmas, Chanukah (this one is tricky because of the silent "c" sound at the beginning of the word), or Kwanzaa.

♥ Name the months that come before and after December.

♥ String popcorn for an outdoor tree and count the kernels of popcorn.

January and February Fun (Ages 3–7)   Your child can:

♥ Count from ten to one while bringing in the New Year (ages 6–7).

♥ Say five words that begin with the same sound heard in the beginning of the word January.

♥ Name the letters in the word January.

♥ Count the number of Sundays in January.

♥ Circle the birthdays of two presidents who were born in the month of February (Lincoln and Washington).

♥ Point to the pictures of Lincoln and Washington on money and name the bills and coins (one-dollar bill, five-dollar bill, penny, and quarter) (ages 6–7).

♥ Count the number of days in January and February. Say which month has more days (ages 6–7).

♥ Trace and cut out hearts for Valentine's Day. (See Appendix 7.)

March and April Surprises (Ages 3–7)   While shaking off Old Man Winter and greeting spring, your child can:

❀ Name objects or things that can be blown by the wind.

❀ Plant a lima bean in a clear plastic cup and watch it grow.

❀ Tell you the number of leaves a clover has.

❀ Circle St. Patrick's Day on the calendar.

❀ Name five things that are green.

❀ Chart the number of rainy and sunny days in April (ages 6–7).

❀ Listen and describe sounds heard outside on a spring morning or afternoon (ages 5–7).

❀ Find and cut out pictures of five different flowers.

❀ Point to the parts of a flower (leaf, stem, petal, and roots) (ages 5–7).

❀ Name items worn on a rainy day.

❀ Circle the word "green" in a magazine or newspaper.

❀ Fly a kite on a windy day (ages 5–7).

May, June, and July Sizzlers (Ages 4–7)   During the hot summer months, your child can:

☀ Name the colors on the flag.

☀ Count the stars and stripes on the flag.

☀ Tell how may red and white stripes make up the flag.

☀ Mark Memorial Day on the calendar.

☀ Count the number of flags he or she sees in a parade.
☀ Name the items needed for a picnic.
☀ Name the colors seen while watching fireworks.
☀ Circle July 4 on the calendar.
☀ Build sandcastles on the beach.
☀ Collect seashells and sort by size and shape.
☀ Listen to the sound of the ocean.

6

BACKYARD AND OUTSIDE TRIVIA

Turn your backyard and surrounding neighborhood into a learning laboratory. No special equipment or scientific tools are needed. All that is required are time and your imagination. Spend endless hours enjoying the marvelous wonders of the outside world. You and your child can:

- Tour your backyard and neighborhood.
- Make mud pies and build tunnels.
- Watch the sunset on a quiet evening.
- Visit the local fire station and post office.
- Count the number of butterflies you see on a sunny afternoon.
- Stroll around the block and count lines in the sidewalk.
- Watch a bumblebee sitting on a flower.
- Listen to the sounds of crickets in the evening.
- Attend a story time or puppet show at the local library.
- Observe the sky at night and find the moon.
- Find pictures in a magazine of the animals, birds, and insects you saw outside.
- Collect different rocks and sort by color, size, and shape.

- Count the trees and fire hydrants you pass during an afternoon walk.
- Measure the width and length of the yard with footsteps.
- Measure around a tree (circumference) with yarn or string.
- Name and point at objects outside representing a circle, triangle, square, and rectangle.
- Plant a small vegetable or flower garden and observe the growth (ages 5–7).
- Count the number of times your child bounces a ball in one minute.
- Skip, gallop, and jump rope around the yard.
- Make figures and objects out of clay.
- Draw or paint a picture of the backyard or the front of the house.
- Make foot- and handprints in sand or dirt.
- Identify sounds you hear outside.
- Plan a pretend tea party for imaginary friends.
- Name shapes and colors seen while outside.
- Describe a house on your street.
- Count and name the signs seen on the street.
- Describe and name the colors on a traffic light. What do the colors tell us to do?
- Say the names of the letters on the street name signs.
- Say the numbers on the houses down the street.

Add more spice to outdoor activities by trying the following games/activities that provide practice for developing skills as well as family fun.

Letter Scavenger Hunt (Ages 5-7) Materials Needed: A pack of unlined 5" × 7" index cards and a black permanent marker or crayons.

Directions: Write (print) a letter of the alphabet on an index card. There should be twenty-six cards. You may write the capital (uppercase) form of the letter on the front of the card and the small (lowercase) form of the letter on the back. Randomly select ten cards and hide them in your backyard. Tell your child to find ten letter cards. Have your child say the name of the letter found and name two items outside that start with the sound made by the letter on the card. Children ages 3–4 may play this game to develop recognition of the letters. After your child finds the letter cards, he or she may try to find the same letters in a book or on a cereal box. Note: Numeral and word cards may be used instead of letter cards for children ages 6–7 as their mathematics and reading skills progress.

I Spy (Ages 5-7) Materials Needed: None. Directions: Make up clues to help your child find and name objects seen or found outside. Say: "I spy something outside that climbs trees and eats acorns. Tell me what I spy." (Answer: squirrel.) See the sample "I Spy" clues below.

1. I fly and build my nest in a tree. (Answer: bird.)
2. I have branches and leaves. (Answer: tree.)
3. The postman/mailman puts mail in me. (Answer: mail box.)
4. I shine brightly during the day. (Answer: sun.)

Note: Encourage six- and seven-year-olds to create their own clues with your assistance.

Weather Watch (Ages 4-7)   Materials Needed: Old calendar and crayons or a fine point, black permanent marker.

Directions: Chart the weather outside by asking your child to tell you how the weather is outside. Use simple symbols to represent windy, sunny, rainy, cold, and cloudy days. (See Appendix 8.) With your assistance, tell your child to select or point to the symbol that tells what the weather is outside. Your child may draw the symbol on the calendar. At the end of each week and/or month, count the number of sunny, rainy, and cloudy days. Also discuss with your child what is appropriate to wear outside for the different kinds of weather.

Nature Walks (Ages 3-7)   Find local nature trails or parks to walk through with your child. Encourage your child to use his or her eyes and ears during your stroll. Stop briefly and ask your child to close his or her eyes and tell you what he or she hears and smells. Walks on nature trails develop a love for the outdoors and an appreciation for nature.

Field Trips (Ages 3-7)   Take every opportunity to turn any place you visit into valuable learning experiences. Children need to visit the library, fire station, police station, zoo, museum, and farm. During your trips ask your child questions about what he or she sees. There are no limits to the places to visit or the questions to ask. Always discuss what was seen or heard with your child. Language goes along with learning and is important for building vocabulary and concepts.

CONCLUDING REMARKS

The key to intellectual development and concept building is exposure. Expose your child to as many activities and experiences as possible. Let your environment and home be your classrooms. The activities and ideas presented in this handbook can serve as a guide and resource. I challenge you to go beyond the materials presented and add additional experiences for your child. Remember you are your child's first and best teacher. Continue on the journey and never lose sight of the integral part you play in your child's intellectual development.

APPENDIX 1

Shoebox Counter

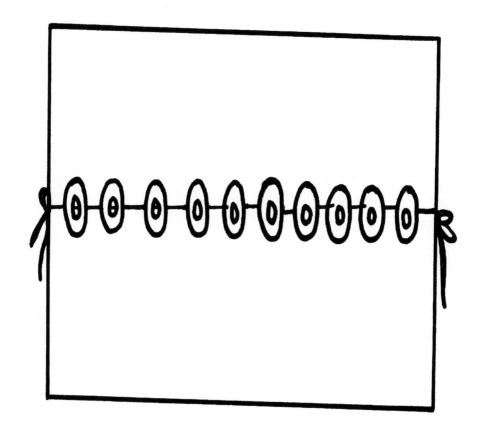

APPENDIX 2

Shoe Tying Board

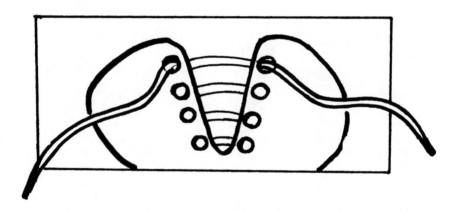

APPENDIX 3

Sound Blending Paper Plate

Chick head
pattern

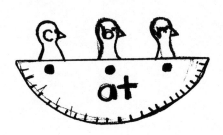

sample

APPENDIX 4

Clothes Hanger Counter

APPENDIX 5

Pumpkin Pattern

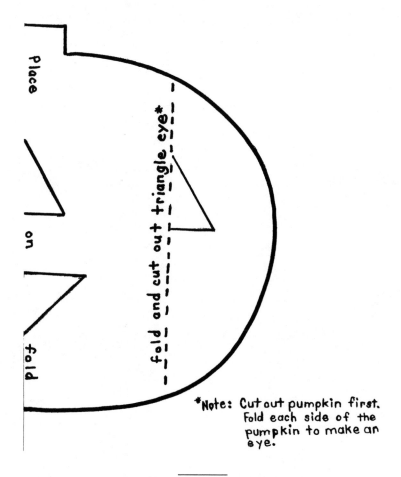

Place on fold

fold and cut out triangle eye*

*Note: Cut out pumpkin first. Fold each side of the pumpkin to make an eye.

APPENDIX 6

Turkey Hand

Trace your child's hand.
Use crayons to color
the feathers and turkey.

APPENDIX 7

Valentine Pattern

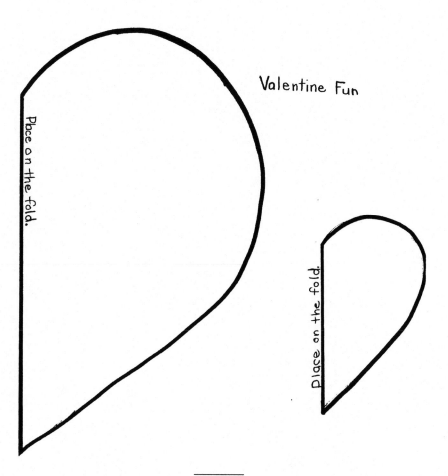

APPENDIX 8

Weather Patterns

BIBLIOGRAPHY AND ADDITIONAL RESOURCES

Armstrong, Thomas. *Awakening Your Child's Natural Genius*. New York: G.P. Putnam's Sons, 1991.

Bredekamp, Sue, editor. *Developmentally Appropriate Practice in Early Childhood Programs Serving Children from Birth through Age 8*. Washington, D.C.: National Association for the Education of Young Children, 1987.

Bredekamp, Sue, and Copple, Carol, eds. *Developmentally Appropriate Practice in Early Childhood Programs*. Washington, D.C.: National Association for the Education of Young Children, 1997.

Helm, Judy H., and Katz, Lillian. *Young Investigators: The Project Approach in the Early Years*. New York: Teachers College Press, Columbia University, 2001.

Marzano, Robert; Pickering, Debra; and Pollock, Jane. *Classroom Instruction that Works: Researched-Based Strategies for Increasing Student Achievement*. Alexandria, Va.: Association for Supervision and Curriculum Development, 2001.

Mayesky, Mary. *Creative Activities for Young Children*, 5th ed. Albany, N.Y.: Delmar Publishers, 1995.

Owocki, Gretchen. *Make Way for Literacy: Teaching the Way Young Children Learn*. Portsmouth, N.H.: Heinemann, 2001.

Schiller, Pam. *Count on Math: Activities for Small Hands and Lively Minds*. Beltsville, Md.: Gryphon House, 1997.

Schiller, Pam. *Creating Readers*. Beltsville, Md.: Gryphon House, 2001.

ABOUT THE AUTHOR

Dr. Sheila E. Sapp, a former elementary school teacher, reading specialist, instructional supervisor, curriculum director, and assistant principal, resides in Woodbine, Georgia, with her husband, Everette. Sapp is currently an elementary principal for the Camden County School System located in Kingsland, Georgia. She is a member of the Georgia Association of Educators, International Reading Association, Georgia International Reading Association, National Association for the Education of Young Children, Georgia Educational Leaders, and the Association for Supervision and Curriculum Development.